Mr Shaha's
MARVELLOUS
MACHINES

Adventures in Making
Round the Kitchen Table

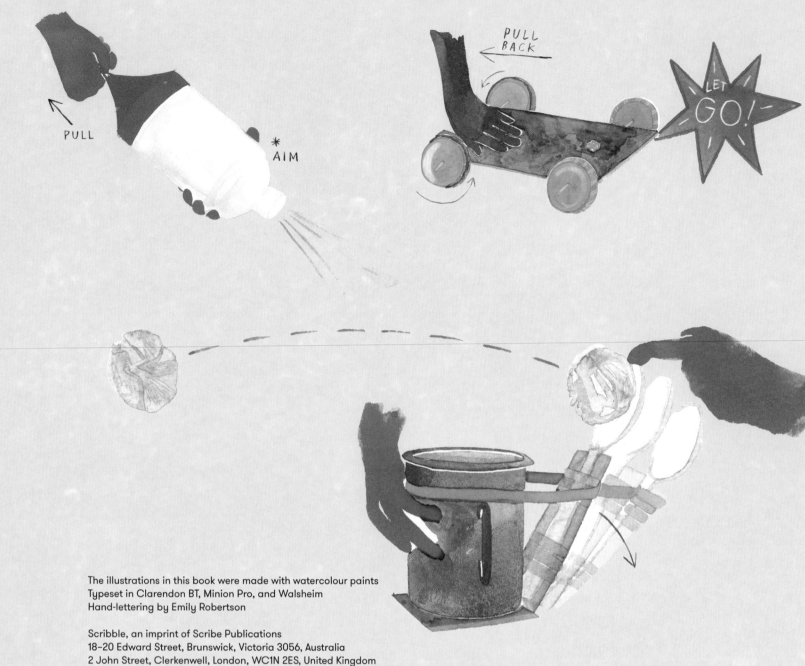

PULL

*AIM

PULL BACK

LET GO!

The illustrations in this book were made with watercolour paints
Typeset in Clarendon BT, Minion Pro, and Walsheim
Hand-lettering by Emily Robertson

Scribble, an imprint of Scribe Publications
18–20 Edward Street, Brunswick, Victoria 3056, Australia
2 John Street, Clerkenwell, London, WC1N 2ES, United Kingdom
3754 Pleasant Ave, Suite 100, Minneapolis, Minnesota 55409 USA

Text copyright © Alom Shaha 2021
Illustrations copyright © Emily Robertson 2021
Based on Sarah Malley's design for *Mr Shaha's Recipes for Wonder*

First published by Scribble in 2021
Reprinted 2021

978 1 922310 03 3 (AU hardback)
978 1 913348 12 0 (UK hardback)

Catalogue records for this title are available from the National Library of Australia and the British Library.

This book is printed with vegetable-soy based inks, on FSC® certified paper and other controlled material from responsibly managed forests, ensuring that the supply chain from forest to end-user is chain of custody certified.
Printed and bound in Poland by OzGraf.

scribblekidsbooks.com

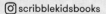 scribblekidsbooks

FSC
www.fsc.org
MIX
Paper from
responsible sources
FSC® C163799

Scribble acknowledges the Wurundjeri Woi Wurrung of the Kulin Nations — the first and continuing custodians of the land on which our books are created. Sovereignty has never been ceded.
We pay our respects to Elders past and present.

Mr Shaha's
MARVELLOUS
MACHINES

Adventures in Making
Round the Kitchen Table

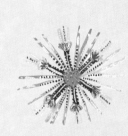

Alom Shaha
and
Emily Robertson

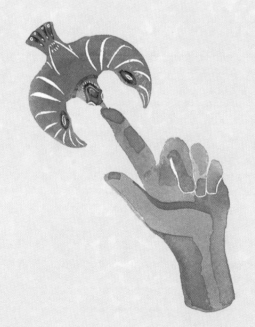

S
SCRIBBLE

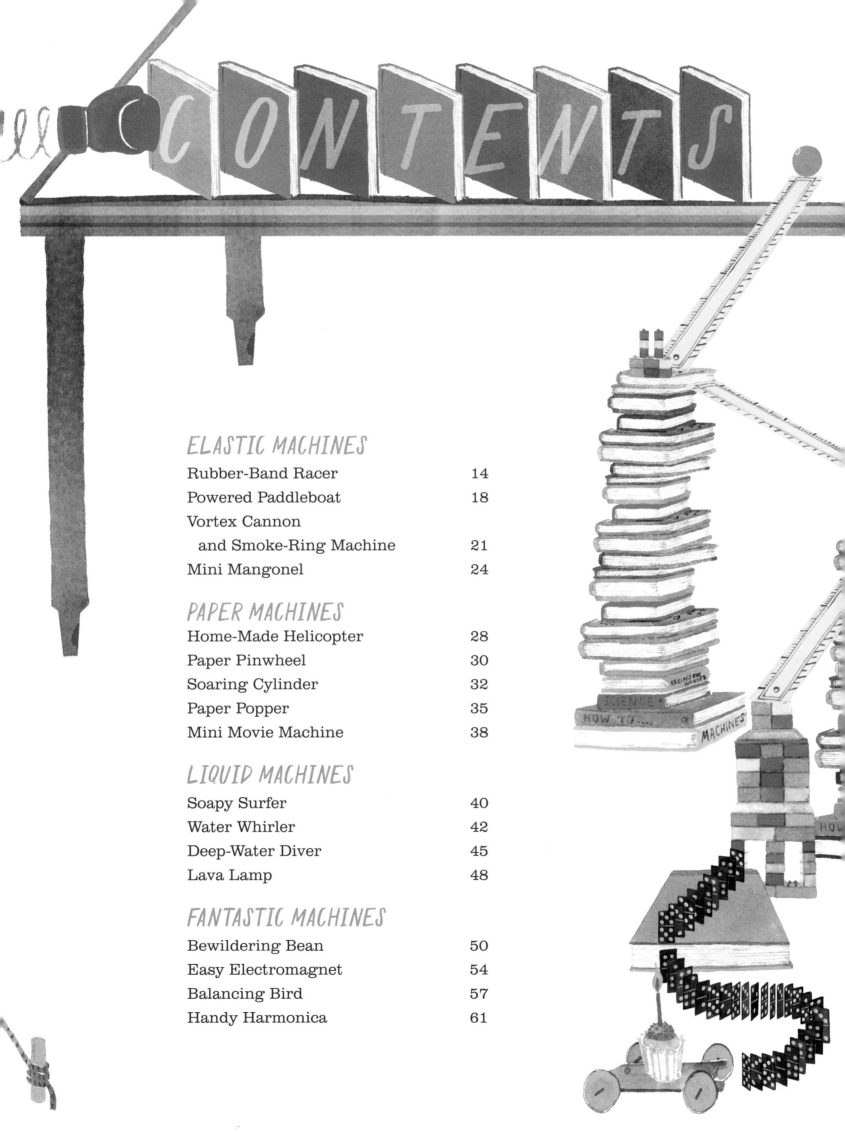

CONTENTS

THE JOY OF MAKING

I was born in a little village in Sylhet, Bangladesh. Back in 1973, there was no electricity or running water, but there were lots of wide-open spaces to run around in, a massive pond to swim in, and no shortage of ways for a child like me to have fun. My family grew most of their own food and made lots of the everyday things they needed for themselves, including clothes, baskets, toothbrushes, and hand fans for keeping them cool. They had to know how to make, mend, and maintain a lot of things, because they didn't have the convenience of supermarkets or the internet. Of course, they had to buy some things, like medicines and the cast-iron water pump at the bottom of the hill, but they were experts at recycling and re-using things like glass bottles and plastic bags, which they couldn't make for themselves.

When I came to England, I missed my grandparents, aunties, uncles, and cousins. But I also missed some of the delicious fruits that used to be abundant, like mangoes, jackfruits, and boroi, a small berry that was deliciously sour when dried. My favourite fruit is the lychee, and once we came to England, it was a real treat to have just three or four of the small, fragrant, juicy fruits a year. I remember going back to Bangladesh as a ten-year-old and feeling like I'd won the lottery when someone handed me a whole bunch of lychees straight from a tree.

There's another reason why I love lychees—they always remind me of an older cousin who showed me something amazing to do

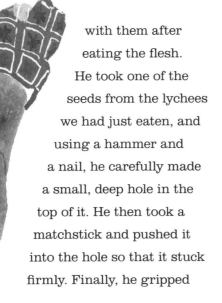

with them after eating the flesh. He took one of the seeds from the lychees we had just eaten, and using a hammer and a nail, he carefully made a small, deep hole in the top of it. He then took a matchstick and pushed it into the hole so that it stuck firmly. Finally, he gripped

the matchstick between his thumb and forefinger and gave it a quick flick, setting the seed whizzing around on the table. He had made a spinning top and shown me my first home-made toy.

A spinning top is a fun and interesting thing to play with, but what I found really special was the way my cousin had taken an everyday object that was destined for the bin and transformed it into something delightful. Over the years, I've come across many other examples of simple toys that can be made from things you might have lying around the house. The joy to be had from such toys isn't just from playing with them, but from making them. It is tremendously satisfying and empowering to make your own rubber-band-powered boat or balancing bird instead of buying it from a shop.

I've included some of my favourite home-made toys as the 'marvellous machines' in this book. Strictly speaking, a 'machine' is something that

CREATIVITY
SCIENTIFIC THINKING
PROBLEM-SOLVING
PRACTICAL SKILLS

does something useful or makes things easier for us, like a car or a vacuum cleaner. But I think that the contraptions and toys in this book provide fun and wonder—and that this also makes them useful. It's not just the finished product that's useful; the process of making these machines, and getting them to do what they're supposed to, will help you understand how they work in a way that simply playing with them wouldn't.

There are other benefits to making things for yourself, including developing your creativity, scientific thinking, problem-solving, and practical skills. I think we all have an innate desire to make things, but often lack the opportunity to do so in the modern world, where so much of what we consume and use is made for us. I don't want to make any promises, but constructing the 'marvellous machines' in this book might just bring you joy in ways you haven't imagined, and make you better equipped to go out and help the world with your own ideas and skills.

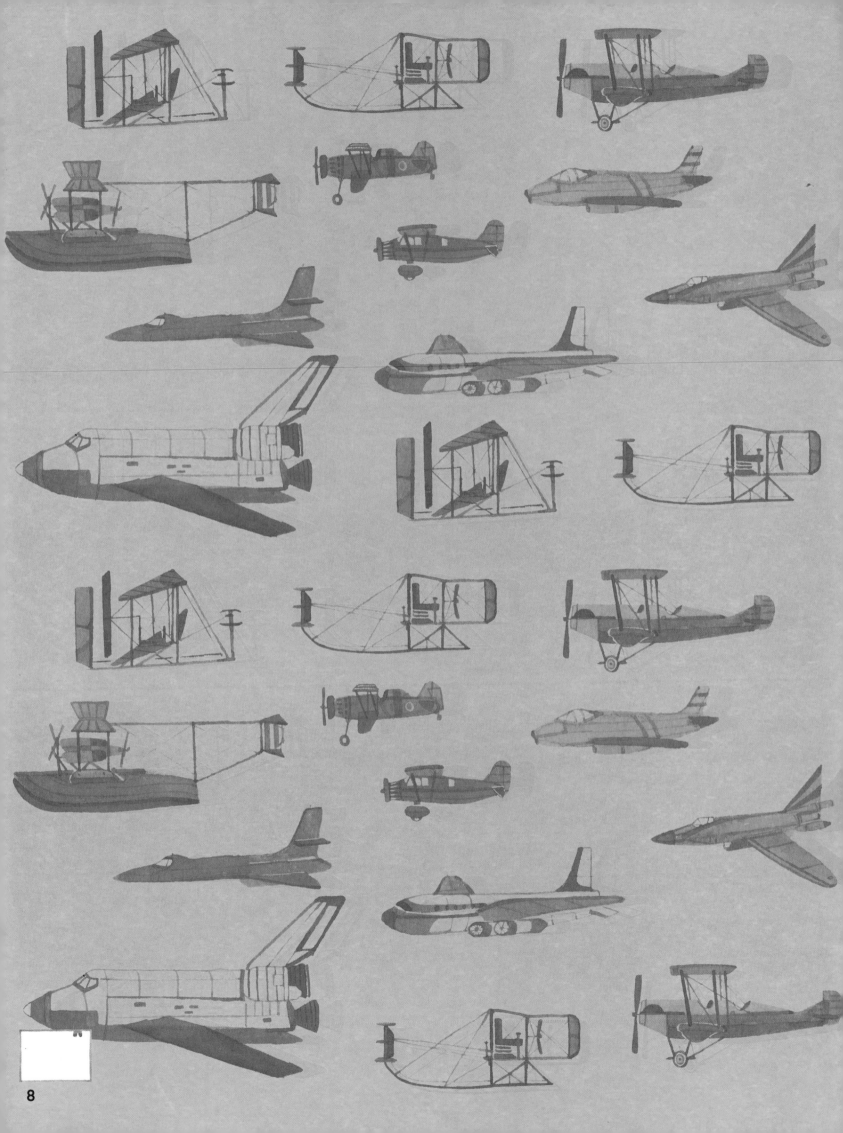

IMPROVE IT!

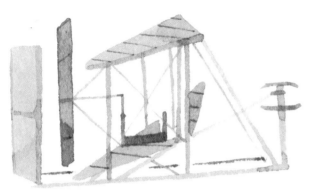

1903 Wright Flyer L.

15th Century Leonardo Da Vinci Flying Machine

A lot of the designs for the machines in this book are very basic. There are two reasons for this:

1 I want to make it as easy as possible for you to make a working machine so you can play and experiment with it.

2 I want you to experience the satisfaction of improving the machines for yourself.

Sometimes we can make a machine better by trial and error, but it's usually more efficient to approach things scientifically. The 'Mr Shaha Says' section of each activity explains the scientific principles behind how a particular machine works. For example, if a machine works by using the stored energy in a twisted rubber band, you might want to think about changing the rubber band in some way, or if something works by producing vibrations, you might want to adjust the thing that is vibrating.

One of the ways to improve a machine might be to change the materials from which it's made or to change its shape and size. When you're doing this, it's a good idea to be scientific in your approach and make sure that you're doing a fair test to find out what change is making the difference you want to your machine. That means only changing one factor at a time (for example, only the size, or shape, or number of rubber bands) while keeping all the other conditions the same.

Finally, one simple way to improve your machines is to decorate them! This might not make them work any better, but real engineers have to think about how things look when they design everything—from aeroplanes to washing machines to mobile phones. Design skills are important for making products and toys easy and safe to use, as well as visually appealing.

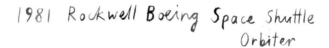

1981 Rockwell Boeing Space Shuttle Orbiter

HOW?

YOU DON'T HAVE TO READ THIS BOOK FROM START TO FINISH – JUST CHOOSE A 'MARVELLOUS MACHINE' YOU LIKE THE LOOK OF AND START MAKING IT. THE INSTRUCTIONS IN THIS BOOK ARE JUST A GUIDE – I HOPE YOU'LL COME UP WITH BETTER WAYS OF DOING THINGS FOR YOURSELF.

WEIGHT
DISTANCE
LENGTH

WHY?

OB
TIN FO
PING-PONG BALL
CEREAL
10p
BUTTON
SHARPENER
TOY PIG

SAFETY

In some of these projects, you will need to use sharp objects and potentially toxic ingredients. These projects should be perfectly safe, so long as you are careful and sometimes get a grown-up to help when you are uncertain or when I suggest this in the instructions. It's more fun to experiment with someone else anyway! When you see this 'BE SAFE' symbol, ask an adult to help you out.

BE SAFE

minds
ON

A NOTE FOR GROWN-UPS

If you're planning on doing one of the activities in this book with a child or children, read the whole section in advance so that you are fully equipped to help them get the most out of it. If you have time, try out the practical elements of an activity on your own first, so that you can maximise its potential for eliciting joy and wonder in children. Most importantly, make use of the suggested questions in the book so that children are 'minds-on' when doing the activity, as well as 'hands-on'. Don't worry if you don't know the answers to the questions yourself—it is the process of asking questions, and trying to work them out together, that will help your child develop and improve the way they think about the world and approach challenges and problems.

ON

ON

RECYCLING AND RE-USE

We're living in a time when the world is running out of resources such as rare-earth metals, and we are increasingly aware of the environmental problems that come with using materials like plastic. One of the advantages of becoming a 'maker' is that you can recycle and re-use materials, which will help tackle these issues. As much as I can, I've tried to use materials for these 'marvellous machines' that you might otherwise be throwing away or recycling. Once you've finished with your machines, you can either keep them or take them apart and put their constituent parts in the recycling or rubbish as appropriate.

10   20   30   40   50   ON
  15   25

CENTIME

1 10 cm
2 24 cm
3 32 cm
4 41·3 cm
5
6

MINDS-ON, AS WELL AS HANDS-ON

Francis Bacon

'A PRUDENT QUESTION IS ONE-HALF OF WISDOM.'

– Francis Bacon, scientist who helped develop the scientific method.

This book is all about making things, so it's definitely a book that's all about being hands-on. But you'll get much more out of each activity if you're also minds-on. This means thinking carefully about what you're doing and what is happening at every stage of the process. One of the best ways to start thinking like a scientist or engineer is to ask good questions as you go along. There are all sorts of questions you could ask, but here are some that I think are particularly 'scientific' because they can usually be answered by observation or experimentation:

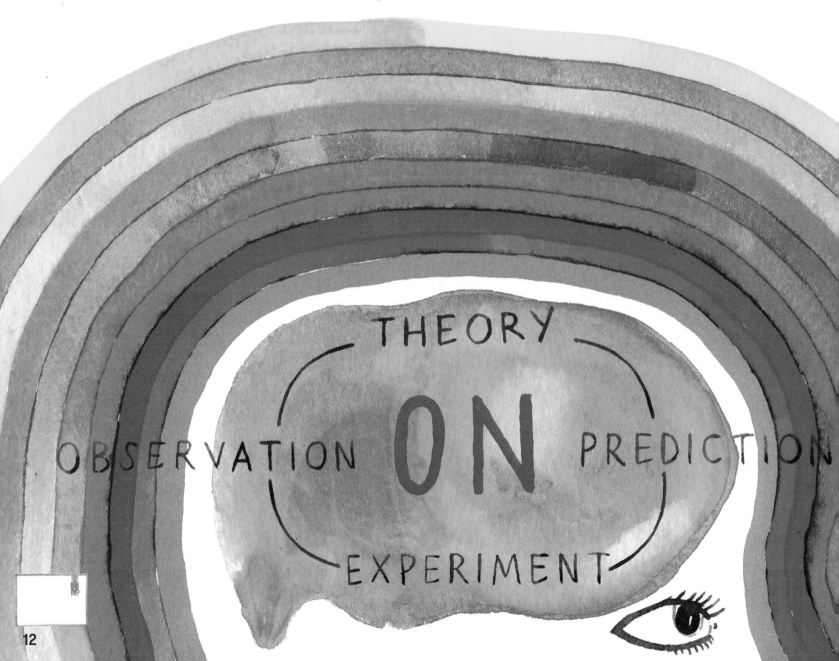

Making and recording measurements	
Before the experiment	How can we measure what's going on?
During the experiment	How can we record our measurements?
Making predictions	
During the experiment	What will happen next?
	What will happen when we add this?
Predicting effects of changes	What will happen if we make this longer/shorter?
	What will happen if we do this again?
Following procedures, describing what happens	
Looking ahead	What does the book say to do next?
	What can we do with this?
Looking back	What did we do first? Next?
	Have we done this bit?
Looking at what happens	What happened when we did this?
	What did you see?
	Was that a surprise?
Making changes	
Changing the experiment	How could we make this bigger? Longer? Heavier? Faster?
	What else could we change?
	Are we doing a 'fair test'? (Are we only changing one thing at a time?)
Making comparisons	
Comparing	Which is bigger? Longer? Heavier? Faster?
	Which took longest? Which was loudest?
Measuring	How much longer is this?
	How long did it take?
Explaining what happens, developing theories	
During the experiment	What makes this move?
	Why doesn't this one sink?
While making changes	Why do you say this one will fall faster?
	What will make this one spin slower?
	What makes you think that?

RUBBER-BAND RACER

PARTS REQUIRED

* Piece of stiff cardboard about 15 cm by 10 cm
* 2 wooden kebab skewers
* 1 drinking straw (kebab skewers must fit through)
* 4 round plastic milk-bottle lids or similar
* Sticky tape
* Scissors
* A lump of plasticine, or blu-tack, or a pencil eraser
* 2 small rubber bands to fit around bottle tops
* 1 long rubber band, at least 15 cm when cut open

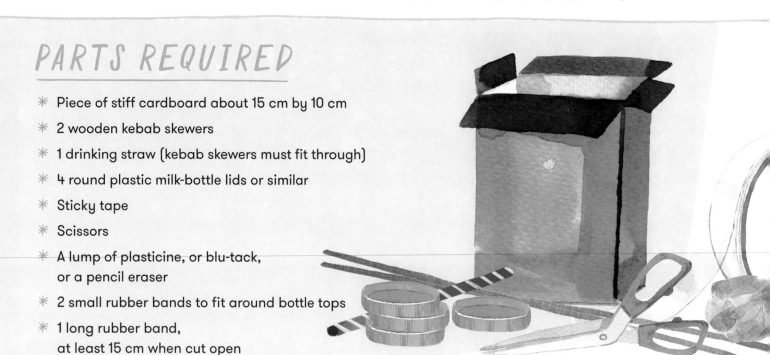

Very few machines have changed the world as much as cars have. On the positive side, they made it much easier for people to travel long distances, and to transport things like food from one place to another. However, cars have also been responsible for producing a lot of pollution and contributing to climate change. Sadly, this rubber-band-powered car isn't the solution to more environmentally friendly transport, but it will provide you with a challenging build and lots of fun if you get it right!

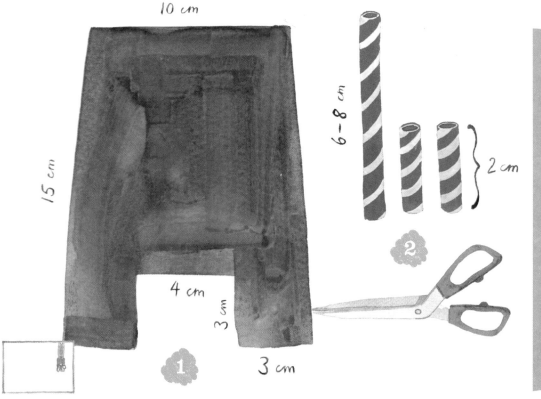

10 cm

15 cm

6–8 cm

2 cm

4 cm

3 cm

3 cm

METHOD

Follow the pictures to build a basic rubber-band-powered car.

1 Cut a notch about 4 cm wide and 3 cm long in the middle of one end of your piece of carboard, as shown.

2 Cut your straw so that you have three little tubes, two of which are 2 cm long and one that is between 6 and 8 cm long.

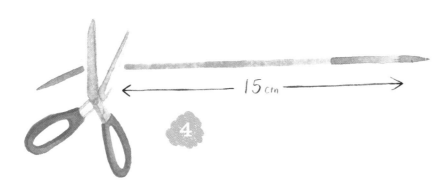

15 cm

4

BOTTOM

3

5

6

7

3 Use sticky tape to attach the straws to the piece of card in the positions shown.

4 Carefully cut or break your skewers so that they are 15 cm or so long, including the pointy end.

5 Use a skewer to make a small hole in the card roughly in the position shown.

6 Cut your long rubber band so that you have a long piece of rubber. This will be your 'motor'.

7 Thread the rubber band through the hole in the card and tie a double or triple knot in it so that it can't be pulled back through the hole easily.

What could you change to make your car go further or faster?

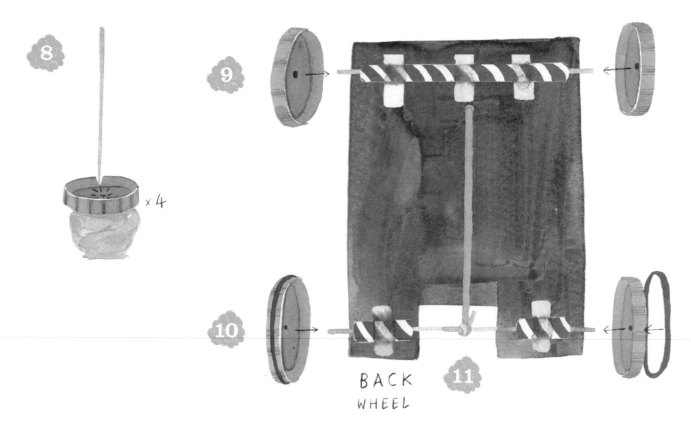

BACK WHEEL

PULL BACK

LET GO!

8 Place a bottle top on top of a lump of plasticine (or blu-tack or eraser) and pierce it using a kebab skewer. Repeat this for each bottle top.

9 Pass the skewers through the straws and fix the wheels on the end.

10 Put a rubber band round each of the back wheels.

11 Tie the loose end of the long piece of rubber to the back skewer.

12 Place your car on a smooth floor (not carpeted) and gently pull it back so that the rubber winds round the back axle of your car.

13 Let go of your car!

What would happen if you used a **thicker or longer** rubber band for the 'motor'?

What would happen if you used **bigger or smaller** wheels?

MR SHAHA says...

When you pull the car back, the rubber band is stretched and stores energy. The more you stretch the rubber band, the more energy is stored. When you release the car, the rubber band unwinds and makes the back axle spin, driving the car forward. Scientists say that energy has been transferred from the elastic potential store of the rubber band to the kinetic energy store of the car.

The wheels at the back of the car spin very quickly when the rubber-band motor unwinds. The rubber bands around the back wheels help them to grip onto the surface the car is on. If you look carefully at what the wheels are doing, you'll see that they push backwards on the floor to make the car move forward.

This is an example of Newton's Third Law in action. The law says that forces always occur in pairs of equal size but

acting in opposite directions. So, if you push something, it will always push back on you with the same amount of force in the opposite direction. The effect of these forces is not always the same, because the forces act on different objects. So, when the car pushes the floor backwards, we don't see the floor move, but we do see the result of the car being pushed forward by the floor.

NEWTON'S THIRD LAW in ACTION

TYRE PUSHES ON ROAD

ROAD PUSHES ON TYRE

POWERED PADDLEBOAT

PARTS REQUIRED

* A large empty juice carton or piece of cardboard from a cereal box or similar
* A rubber band (a thin, stretchy one is best)
* Scissors
* Glue stick
* Sticky tape
* A bath or large tub filled at least 10 cm deep with water

There are lots of ways to get a boat to move across the water—rowing boats use human power, sailboats use the power of the wind, and motorboats use engines to power them. In the nineteenth century and early twentieth century, passenger ships were usually powered by steam, which turned large paddle wheels to move the ships quickly across the oceans. Make your own rubber-band-powered paddleboat and see how far, or how fast, you can make it go.

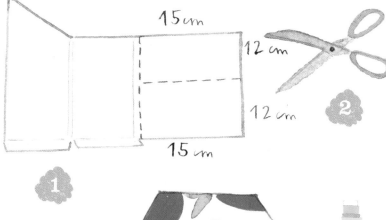

METHOD

1 Cut open your empty juice carton and open it up so you have a flat piece of material.

2 Cut out two rectangles that measure 12 cm by 15 cm. Use the glue stick to stick the two rectangles together firmly to make a thicker rectangle. Wait until the glue is dry before doing the next step.

3 Cut out a 6-cm-by-6-cm slot so you are left with the shape shown in the illustrations.

(If you are using ordinary cardboard instead of a juice carton, cover the shape in sticky tape to make it waterproof.)

4 From the leftover card, cut out four rectangular strips of card measuring 4 cm by 6 cm. (Again, cover these in sticky tape if you are not using card from a juice carton.)

5 Fold each of these strips in half lengthways, then unfold them so that you are left with 'L' shaped pieces of card.

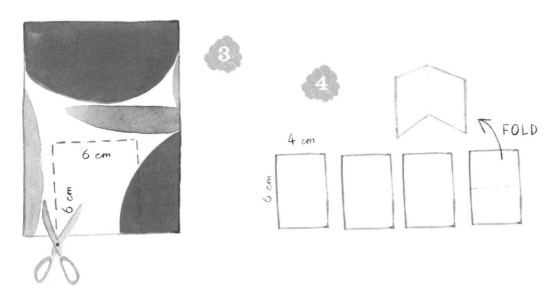

3

4

6 cm

6 cm

4 cm

6 cm

FOLD

Does it matter how **wide or long** the paddles are?

Could you make the boat go **faster or slower** by changing its shape or size?

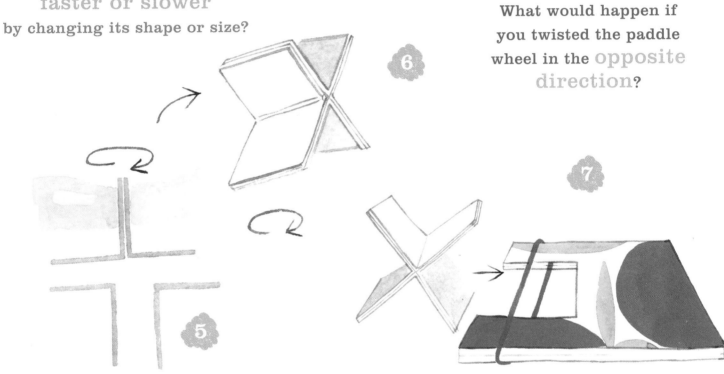

5

6

What would happen if you twisted the paddle wheel in the **opposite direction**?

7

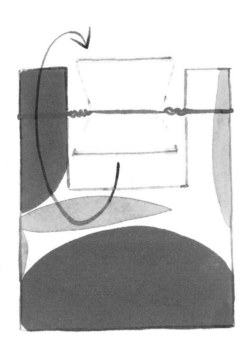

8

6 Use tape to stick the 'L' shapes together to make your paddle wheel, as shown.

7 Stretch your elastic band across the hole at the back of the 'boat'.

8 Insert one of the paddle flaps into the rubber band and twist the rubber band away from the boat several times.

9 Hold the paddle in place so the rubber band doesn't unwind, and put your boat into water.

10 Release the paddle!

How could you make the boat **travel further** before it comes to a stop?

MR SHAHA says...

Twisting the rubber band stretches it, and stores energy. When the rubber band is released, the stored energy is transferred to the paddle wheel, making it spin.

As each blade of the paddle moves through the water, it pushes water away from the boat. This makes the boat move forward in much the same way that you move forward when you use your arms and legs to push water backwards when you swim.

This is a demonstration of a principle that scientists call Newton's Third Law, which says that forces always occur in pairs of equal size but acting in opposite directions. If you push something, it will always push back on you with the same amount of force — but it's important to remember that the effect of these forces is not always the same because the forces act on different objects. Can you think of other examples of moving things that rely on Newton's Third Law?

VORTEX CANNON AND SMOKE-RING MACHINE

PARTS REQUIRED

* A 1-litre plastic drink bottle
* A balloon
* Sticky tape and scissors
* Some pieces of tissue or scrap paper
* An incense stick or cone (optional)

BE SAFE

BE SAFE

The activity involves cutting a plastic bottle and (optionally) using burning incense. Please get an adult to help you with these parts of the project.

In the story of The Three Little Pigs, a wolf is able to blow down two of the pigs' houses by huffing and puffing. It may seem unlikely that a puff of air could do much damage to a solid structure like a house, but making this vortex cannon will show you just how the wolf might have been able to accomplish his terrible feats.

METHOD

1 Carefully cut off the bottom of the bottle.

2 Tie the neck of the uninflated balloon.

3 Cut the bottom quarter or so of the balloon off, as shown.

4 Open out the balloon and stretch it over the open bottom of the bottle, so that it forms a tight 'skin'.

5 Wrap a couple of loops of sticky tape firmly around the edge of the rubber so that it makes an airtight seal with the bottle.

6 Place your tissue or scraps of paper on the table to make a target.

21

7 Point the open end of your cannon at your target and fire it by pulling back on the balloon knot and letting go.

How could you test **how far** the air travels from your cannon?

PULL

* AIM

BE SAFE

TO TURN YOUR VORTEX CANNON INTO A SMOKE-RING MACHINE:

1 Light an incense stick or cone.

2 Hold the open neck of the bottle directly above the burning incense until the bottle is filled with lots of smoke.

3 Point the cannon away from you and give the balloon on the end a gentle tap or poke with your fingers. If you don't get a smoke ring, try tapping or poking a bit harder.

How precisely can you **target something** with your cannon?

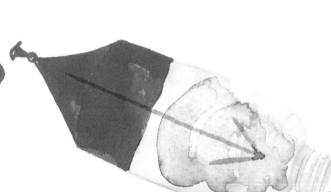

How could you make your cannon **more powerful**?

What is **the heaviest thing** you can knock down with a puff of air from your cannon?

* TOROIDAL VORTEX

Stretching and releasing the rubber balloon pushes a puff of air out of the bottle, which acts as the 'bullet' for your cannon. As it comes out of the bottle, the outside of the puff is slowed down by friction with the bottle neck, while air in the middle of the puff continues to move ahead more quickly.

The slower-moving air on the outside of the puff starts spinning because it is being dragged forward by the faster air in the middle, at the same time as being pulled backwards by frictional forces. The spinning air forms a doughnut shape, also known as a 'toroidal vortex'. You can see this if you use the vortex cannon as a smoke-ring maker.

The ring-shaped 'bullet' of air stays together due to something scientists call the law of conservation of angular momentum, which means that spinning objects tend to stay spinning unless an external force is applied. If it was not spinning, it would quickly spread out into the rest of the air and would not be so good for firing at a target.

23

MINI MANGONEL

PARTS REQUIRED

* A plastic or tin cup
* A dessert spoon (preferably plastic)
* A piece of scrap cardboard — at least as wide as the bottom of your cup and twice as long
* 1 or more rubber bands
* Different types of rubber band (optional)
* A projectile like a table-tennis ball or piece of scrunched-up aluminium foil
* Scissors
* Sticky tape or masking tape

Sadly, not all machines are designed for peaceful purposes. A mangonel is a type of catapult that was used to fire large rocks at castles during sieges. The word 'mangonel' is derived from the Greek, meaning 'engine of war', but this mini version was devised by my friend Jonathan Sanderson to help you investigate what factors affect the distance that it will throw a projectile.

METHOD

1 Cut a square of cardboard so that it covers the bottom of your cup.

2 Use a long piece of tape to stick the cardboard square to the bottom of your cup.

3 Cut another square the same size as the first one, then cut it in half to make a rectangle.

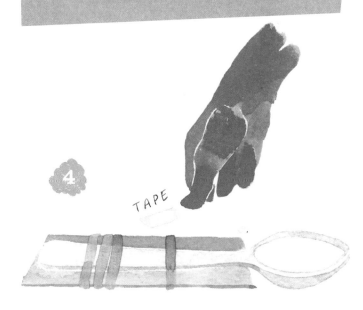

TAPE

TAPE

MAKE A HINGE

4 Stick the cardboard rectangle to the handle of your spoon, wrapping the sticky tape around a couple of times to make it really secure. Alternatively, you could use small rubber bands to hold the spoon in place.

5 Cut a length of tape and use it to make a hinge attaching the card with the spoon to the card on the mug, as shown.

6 Stand the cup up and slip a rubber band over the top.

7 Hold the table-tennis ball or your ball of scrunched-up kitchen foil in the spoon, pull it back, and fire!

What things could you change to make the projectile go further?

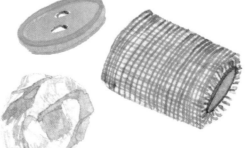

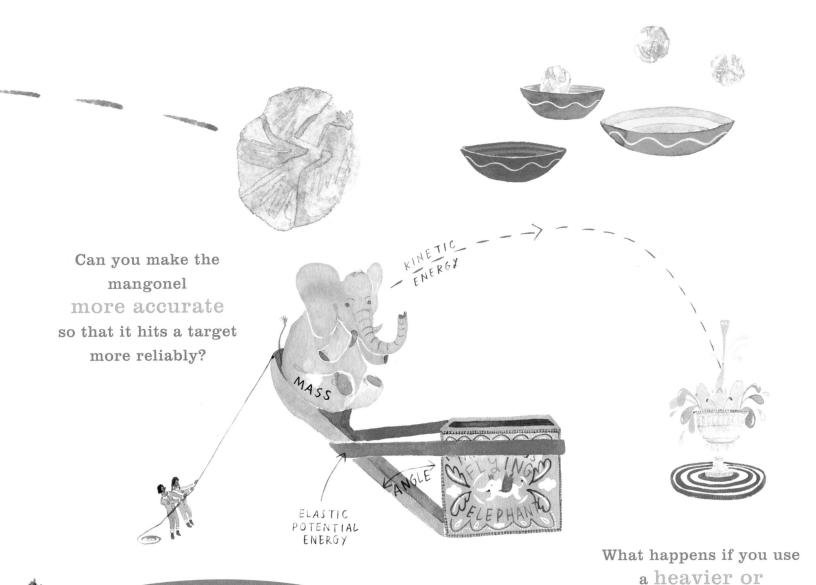

Can you make the mangonel **more accurate** so that it hits a target more reliably?

What happens if you use a **heavier or lighter** projectile?

MR SHAHA says...

A projectile is any object that is fired through the air. The mangonel, like all catapults, allows you to give more energy to a projectile than you normally could just by throwing it. When you pull the spoon back, energy is transferred from you and stored in the elastic band, as long as it remains stretched. Scientists say that the elastic band now has elastic potential energy. In actual mangonels, the energy was stored in twisted ropes that were pulled tight by one or more soldiers pulling with all their might. Releasing the elastic band transfers the energy to the projectile, which then has what scientists call 'kinetic' energy because it is moving.

You can store more energy by stretching an elastic band further, or by using a stiffer elastic band. If stretched by the same amount, a stiffer elastic band will store more energy than one that is easy to stretch.

The distance that a projectile travels depends on its mass, the amount of energy it's given (and so the speed at which it leaves the catapult), and the angle at which it's launched. It also depends on the strength of gravity, but we can ignore that since the strength of gravity is pretty much the same everywhere on the surface of the earth.

HOME-MADE HELICOPTER

PARTS REQUIRED

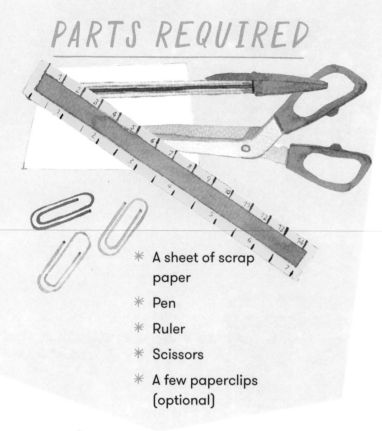

* A sheet of scrap paper
* Pen
* Ruler
* Scissors
* A few paperclips (optional)

One of my favourite things in autumn is finding 'helicopter seeds' from Sycamore trees and throwing them up in the air to watch them spiral down. Winged seeds like these have evolved in order to disperse as far as possible from the tree that produced them. As you'll see from this activity, the whirling allows seeds to stay in the air for longer so that the wind can carry them further. They are a great example of how there are 'marvellous machines' in the natural world from which we can take inspiration.

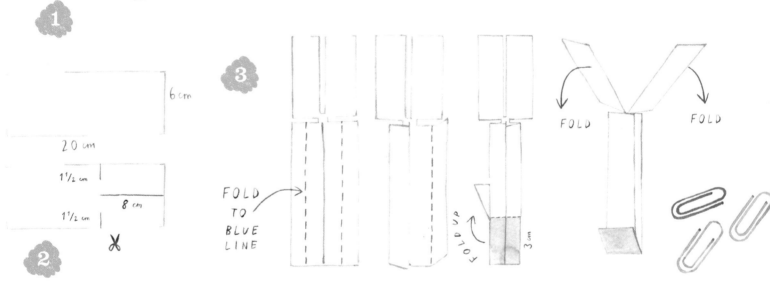

METHOD

1 Cut a rectangle of paper that is 6 cm by 20 cm.

2 Make three cuts in the paper as shown on the red lines above.

3 Fold the paper as shown.

4 Hold the helicopter by the bottom and drop it from as high as you can. (You could decorate the helicopter before doing this.)

5 If you have any, try adding one or more paperclips to the bottom of the helicopter.

Can you **describe** what happens when you **drop** the helicopter?

What happens if you **change** the **direction** in which the blades are folded at the top? (Look carefully at the way the helicopter spins.)

4

What could you change to try and make a helicopter that falls as **slowly as possible**?

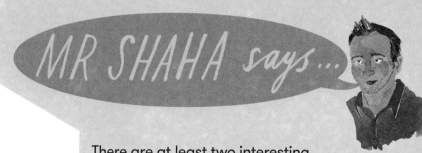

MR SHAHA says...

There are at least two interesting questions to try and answer about the helicopter — why does it spin, and how does the spinning help slow down its fall through the air? The answer to both questions comes down to the two main forces acting on the helicopter — its weight (due to gravity) and the force of the air particles that hit it as it moves.

As the helicopter falls, due to the force of gravity, air pushes up against the blades and hits the corner where the blades meet the stem. This produces an upward force on the blades and a sideways push on each side of the stem. Each blade is attached to one half of the stem, and on opposite sides. This asymmetric design means that the stem has a force acting on both sides of the stem, but not along the same line, and in opposite directions. These unbalanced forces make the whole thing spin, a bit like the way you have to push a coin from one side and pull it from the other if you want to spin it on a table.

The air pushing up on the blades makes them bend up a little, so that they are not horizontal as they spin through the air. As the slanted, spinning blades move through the air, a 'lift' force is produced, which has the result of reducing the effect of gravity on the helicopter. This means the helicopter falls more slowly than it would if it wasn't spinning. You can experience this lift force yourself if you carefully put your hand out of the window of a moving car and angle your palm upwards in the direction you're travelling — you'll feel your hand being pushed up.

29

PAPER PINWHEEL

PARTS REQUIRED

* 1 sharp pencil with eraser on top
* 1 square of scrap paper, roughly 15 cm by 15 cm
* 1 drawing pin
* Eraser
* Scissors
* Ruler

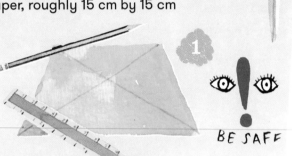

BE SAFE

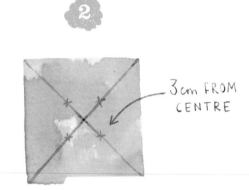

3 cm FROM CENTRE

Humans have used windmills to harness the power of the wind for hundreds of years. They have been used to grind grain, pump water, and generate electricity. There are many designs and shapes that have been tried to find a way to maximise the amount of energy that can be captured from the wind. Making this simple paper pinwheel will allow you to investigate some of the factors that affect how well a windmill works.

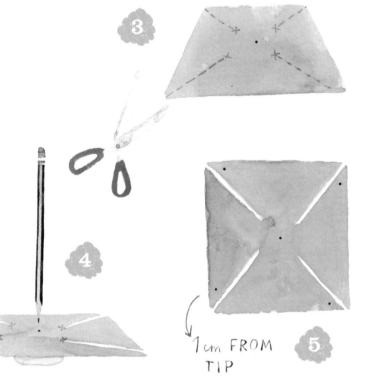

1 cm FROM TIP

METHOD

1 Using your pencil and ruler, mark the diagonals on your piece of paper.

2 Make a mark on each line at 3 cm from the centre, where the lines cross over.

3 Cut the paper along the lines, stopping at the 3 cm mark.

4 Place the centre of your paper on top of your eraser. Using the sharp tip of your pencil, make a small hole in the middle of your square of paper.

5 In the same way, make a small hole about 1 cm away from the tip of one of the cut corners of your square.

6 Repeat this with every alternating corner so that you end up with five holes in total — one in the middle, and one at four of the corners.

FOLD

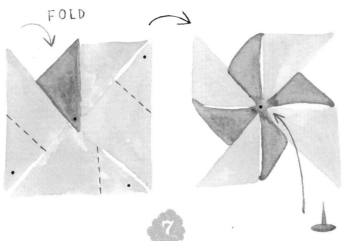

What would happen if the pinwheel had **more blades**?

7

8

7 Curl up the four corners so that their holes line up, and push the drawing pin through these holes and then through the hole in the middle of the paper.

8 Carefully push the drawing pin halfway into the eraser at the top of your pencil. It should be stuck firmly, but still allow the pinwheel to spin freely.

9 Blow on your pinwheel to make it spin, or hold the pencil up with the pinwheel facing forward and go for a walk!

BLOW

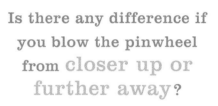

Is there any difference if you blow the pinwheel from **closer up or further away**?

MR SHAHA says...

The pinwheel spins because its overall shape, and the orientation of the individual blades, means that air bounces off it and pushes it in such a way that the whole thing experiences a turning force in one direction. If you blow the front of the pinwheel, the blades are angled such that each blade is pushed in the same direction — so they all spin together.

The pinwheel also has four 'pockets' that can catch the air. If you blow at it from the side,

air goes into these pockets and pushes on the paper, making the wheel turn.

If you blow the back of the pinwheel from some distance, you can see that the air will bounce off the blades, making it go in a particular direction. But if you blow the back of it from close up, the air flows into the cups from behind and makes the pinwheel spin in the opposite direction.

SOARING CYLINDER

PARTS REQUIRED

* 1 piece of A5 paper
  (A4 paper cut in half across its width)
* Sticky tape or glue stick
* Ruler (optional)
* 1 straight-sided glass, mug, or bottle.

What would happen if you made the front of your **cylinder heavier**? How could you do this without adding any more folds?

There are numerous sports that are based on the simple joy of throwing something. Some games, like basketball, darts, and boules, require skill at throwing something at a target, whereas others, like javelin, discus, and shot put, can be won simply by hurling the object as far as possible. If you make it correctly, and get the throwing technique just right, the soaring cylinder will surprise you with just how far you can throw a piece of paper.

FOLD
1½ cm

A5

FOLD AGAIN
x3

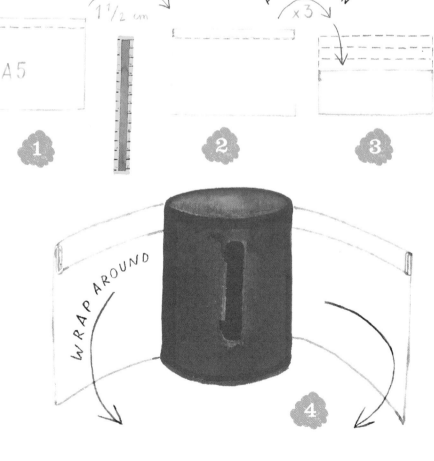

WRAP AROUND

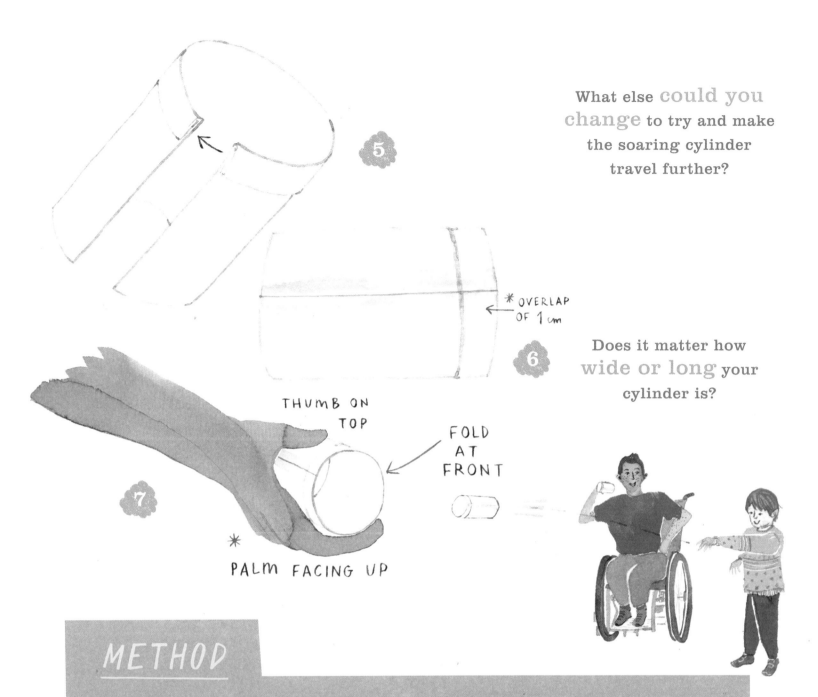

5

6

What else could you change to try and make the soaring cylinder travel further?

Does it matter how wide or long your cylinder is?

* OVERLAP OF 1 cm

THUMB ON TOP

FOLD AT FRONT

7

* PALM FACING UP

METHOD

1 Carefully make a straight fold along the long edge of the paper about 1 1/2 cm wide (you can use a ruler to help with this).

2 Fold this over again, trying to keep the folds as closely lined up as possible.

3 Do this three more times, so that you end up with a heavy 'rim' on one side of the paper.

4 Wrap the paper around the curve of your glass, mug, or bottle, pressing down on the folded paper to make it curved.

5 Bring the paper together into a cylinder and slot one end of the folded rim into the other so that you have an overlap of about 1 cm.

6 Use either sticky tape or glue to stick the paper so that it holds the cylinder together.

7 To throw the cylinder and make it soar (it's best to do this outdoors or in a big hall):

- Hold the cylinder with the palm of your hand upwards and the heavy side of the cylinder facing forward

- Throw the cylinder straight forward in an 'underarm' motion, giving it a little flick to make it spin as it leaves your hand. This can take some practice, but it's worth it!

- Alternatively, if you know how to throw a rugby ball or American football, you can try throwing the cylinder like one of those.

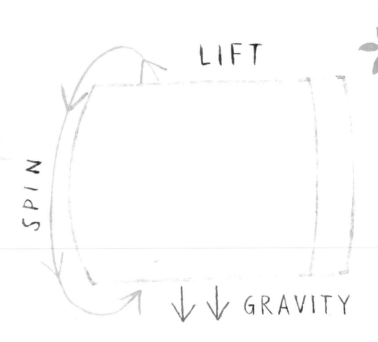

LIFT

SPIN

↓↓ GRAVITY

AIR
RESISTANCE ↑↓ GRAVITY

MR SHAHA says...

With a bit of practice, it's possible to get the soaring cylinder to fly in a surprisingly straight line and for quite some distance. If you throw an object through the air without giving it a spin, it will usually follow a curved path back to the ground. This is because, once it leaves your hand, a thrown object only has two main forces acting on it: gravity and air resistance. Gravity is the force that pulls the object to the ground, and air resistance slows it down as it moves forward.

For an object to 'fly' through the air, it must have a force on it that acts upwards, against gravity. Scientists call this force 'lift', and it can be produced in a variety of ways. The soaring cylinder produces lift because of the way its front rim moves through the air. The top and bottom surfaces of the cylinder behave a bit like aeroplane wings, pushing down on the air and being pushed back up in return.

The key to the cylinder's stability as it flies through the air is the spin you give it as it leaves your hand. Spinning objects tend to stay spinning in the same orientation and resist any forces which try to change that. This is why a spinning top will stay upright while it is spinning, and why it's easy to balance on a bicycle once you've got it moving.

PAPER POPPER

PARTS REQUIRED

* 1 sheet of A4 paper
* Other types of paper from magazines, newspapers, and so on (optional)

My favourite thing about Christmas crackers and party poppers is the noise they make. In both these devices, the sound comes from a small explosion caused by a chemical reaction. If, like me, you're disappointed that crackers often don't 'crack' properly, and you worry that party poppers are wastefully made of plastic, then you'll love this paper popper that can make a surprisingly loud bang—and can be used over and over again.

METHOD

1 Take your sheet of paper and fold it according to the steps shown here.

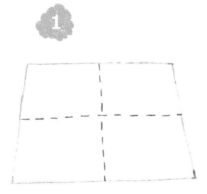

FOLD IN HALF BOTH WAYS AND OPEN FLAT

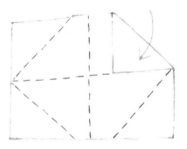

FOLD EACH CORNER IN, LINING THEM UP WITH THE HALFWAY FOLDS

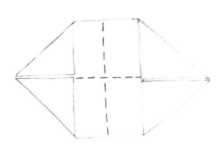

SHOULD LOOK LIKE THIS

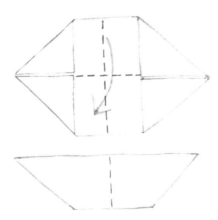

FOLD TOP HALF DOWN TO LINE UP WITH BOTTOM HALF

FOLD HALF OF THE LONG EDGE DOWN TO MEET THE MIDDLE FOLD LINE, THEN FOLD OTHER HALF DOWN

SHOULD LOOK LIKE THIS

FOLD IN HALF AWAY FROM YOURSELF TO MAKE A TRIANGLE

FINISHED!

LOOSE END

HOLD AT LOOSE END

2 Hold the triangle by the two loose ends so that the flaps are pointing away from you.

3 Hold the popper above your head and then bring it down with a quick flick of your arm. It may take some practice to get a loud bang, or you may need to get an adult to do it for you because the popper needs to be moved very quickly to work properly.

POP!

BE SAFE

Don't use the paper popper near anyone's ears or in a room with anyone who is likely to be upset by the noise. Stay away from furniture or any other objects you could hit when swinging your arm to operate the popper.

Do you think the size of the paper will make a difference to the sound the popper makes?

Does the speed at which you flick the popper make a difference to how loud it is?

Does the thickness or type of paper make a difference?

MR SHAHA says...

We hear sounds because our ear contains an eardrum and tiny bones that vibrate when sound waves come into contact with them. Our brains convert these vibrations into what we hear.

Sound waves in the air are produced when the gas particles in the air are made to vibrate (repeatedly move backwards and forwards) and this vibration is passed on from one particle to the next. Unlike waves on the surface of water, sound waves don't go up and down, but move backwards and forwards in the same direction that the wave is moving.

The design of the paper popper means that when you flick it, air quickly fills the pocket behind the flap in the middle. This causes a build-up of pressure in the pocket that makes it pop open suddenly, in the same way an umbrella will flip inside out in windy weather. When this happens, the flap rapidly squashes the air in front of it, a bit like if you punched a springy cushion or mattress. When the air bounces back, it causes the air around it to vibrate, making lots of sound waves that travel away from the popper and into the ears of anyone nearby.

MINI MOVIE MACHINE

PARTS REQUIRED

* A small notebook, or a pad of sticky notes, or some sheets of blank paper

* Pen or pencil

* Scissors

* Glue or staples (if you don't have a notebook or sticky notes)

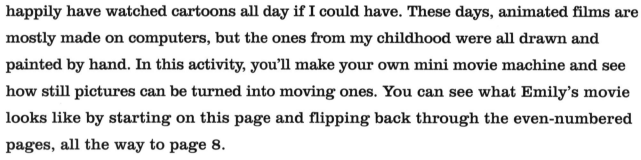

I have always loved cartoons. I grew up in a time when there were only three television channels and they only showed cartoons at certain times of the day, so watching them was a real treat. I would happily have watched cartoons all day if I could have. These days, animated films are mostly made on computers, but the ones from my childhood were all drawn and painted by hand. In this activity, you'll make your own mini movie machine and see how still pictures can be turned into moving ones. You can see what Emily's movie looks like by starting on this page and flipping back through the even-numbered pages, all the way to page 8.

Can you work out how you could make a
stop-motion animation of one of your dolls or
action figures by using photographs instead of drawings?

METHOD

1 If you don't have a notebook or pad of sticky notes, make your own notebook by sticking or stapling 20 small sheets of paper together, making sure the edges are lined up neatly. (If you're using A4 paper, cut it neatly into quarters first.)

2 To make a movie of a sprinting cheetah, you can copy the pictures Emily has drawn onto the pages of your notebook. If you prefer to draw your own moving object, make sure to slightly change the picture, or its position, or both, on each page. Keep your drawing towards the right-hand side of the page. It helps to press down firmly on the paper with your pen so you can see where you drew the previous image when you turn the page.

3 Flip through your book to watch your mini movie. You may need to practise doing this to get the right technique for seeing every page.

4 Once you've made your first simple movie, make more! Include colours, scenery, more than one moving object, or anything else you want.

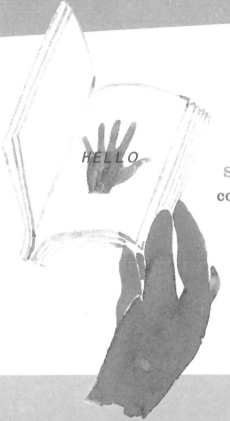

What kind of **special effects** could you include in your movie?

MR SHAHA says...

The mini movie machine creates an optical illusion — it makes you think you're seeing something that's moving, when actually you are seeing a series of still images one after the other. The illusion works partly because your eyes and brain keep hold of whatever you're looking at for a fraction of a second, even after it's no longer in view. This is called 'persistence of vision' and is why, if you flip through your book quickly enough, the pictures merge into one another and seem to change continuously, so you don't see each image on its own as you would if you turned the pages slowly.

For the illusion to work, you usually need to flip through at least ten pages a second. Cinemas usually show films that have 24 'frames per second', which means there are 24 individual images for every second of the film you see. Televisions work in the same way, with the image changing around 25 times a second.

You can experience persistence of vision in another way by doing this simple activity: close one eye and place your hands over the other eye so that there is a small slit you can see through. Look at something far away, perhaps through a window. You shouldn't be able to see much out the slit. Now quickly shake your head from side to side while looking through the slit and you should get a much wider view of whatever it is that you're looking at.

SOAPY SURFER

PARTS REQUIRED

* Washing-up liquid
* Water
* 1 empty juice carton or plastic milk bottle
* 1 matchstick, toothpick, or cotton bud
* 1 baking tray or other large shallow tray

Soap is one of the most useful chemicals in the house. You probably use it at home every day and give little thought to why it's so useful for cleaning with, and how it manages to get rid of dirt and grime that you'd struggle to clean off with just water. This activity makes use of the way soap affects water to do something that looks like magic, and which you can use to create a great racing game if you're feeling competitive.

METHOD

1 Cut your empty juice carton or plastic milk bottle so that you have a flat piece of material that is about 2 cm by 3 cm. Cut one end of this into a point so you have a surfboard shape. You can decorate this if you like.

2 Fill your tray with cold water.

3 Carefully place your surfboard onto the water so that it is floating at one end of the tray.

4 Dip the end of your matchstick into washing-up liquid.

5 To make the surfboard go, touch the water behind it with the soapy end of your matchstick. This can be repeated several times but will eventually stop working. When this happens, simply change the water in your tray.

What happens if you use hot water instead of cold?

Could you make the surfboard go faster or slower by changing its shape or size?

MR SHAHA says...

Adding soap to the water changes its surface in a way that propels the surfboard forward. To see what is going on, start with a fresh tray of water and sprinkle some ground pepper or dried herbs over the surface. Take your soapy matchstick and touch the surface of the water in the middle of the plate — you should see that the pepper or herbs dramatically move away from the point where the soap touches the water.

This happens because the surface of water is a bit like the surface of an inflated balloon and the soap acts like a pin bursting the balloon. In a balloon, every bit of the rubber is pulling on every bit around it. The surface of water is similar, because every molecule is pulling on every other molecule around it, forming a kind of web of molecules. Scientists call the way the water molecules pull on each other 'surface tension'.

When you stick a pin in a balloon, the rubber at that point is broken and the rest of the balloon pulls away from that point. Similarly, when you put soap on the surface of water, it weakens the pull that the water molecules have on each other at that point, breaking the surface tension, so the water molecules are pulled away from that point, taking the surfboard with it.

WATER WHIRLER

PARTS REQUIRED

* 2 large plastic drink bottles (colourless and clear 2-litre bottles work best)
* Sticky tape
* Scissors
* Water from the tap
* Food colouring (optional)
* Cooking oil (optional)

The words 'cyclone' and 'tornado' make me think of dramatic swirls of wind rushing around, destroying everything in their paths. But they don't always have to be dangerous—you can often see the same sort of thing when the wind makes leaves whirl around on the ground. Scientists call a spinning mass of air or water a 'vortex'. Water spinning as it goes down the plughole in the bath is also a vortex. In this activity you'll make your own water whirler to let you observe and investigate vortices (this is the plural of 'vortex'!).

METHOD

1 Remove any labels from the bottles if you can.

2 Using scissors, very carefully cut off the plastic rings at the necks of the bottles.

OFF

BE SAFE

What happens if you spin the bottles in the opposite direction?

2/3 FULL

4

＊ WRAP TIGHT!

BEND LEAKS WOBBLE ✗

3 Pour water into one of the bottles until it is about two-thirds full. Add a few drops of food colouring if you have it.

4 Place the empty bottle on top of the first bottle and carefully wrap sticky tape round their necks several times to join them together. It helps to pull tightly on the sticky tape as you go around, pressing it firmly against the bottle necks to ensure you get a watertight seal.

Does the water flow out of the bottle more quickly when you spin the bottle? How could you check?

FLIP

6

5 Make sure that the empty bottle on top is stuck firmly to the other bottle — the joint you've made should not wobble or bend when you move the bottom bottle from side to side.

6 Pick your water whirler up by the middle,

as shown in the picture, and very carefully and slowly turn it upside down and watch what happens.

7 Turn the bottles upside down again, but this time, give them a quick spin before you put them down.

43

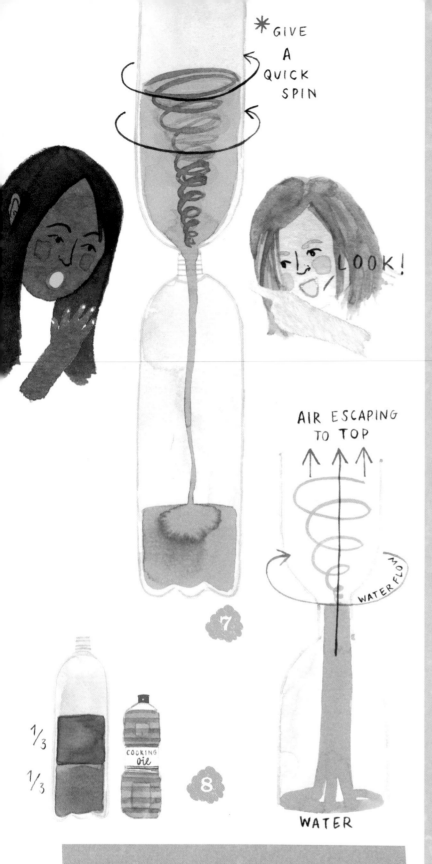

*GIVE A QUICK SPIN

LOOK!

AIR ESCAPING TO TOP

WATER FLOW

7

8

1/3
1/3

COOKING oil

WATER

8 OPTIONAL: Disconnect your bottles from each other and replace one-third of the water with cooking oil. Reconnect the tubes. What do you think will happen when you try steps 6 and 7 again?

Does it matter how many times you spin the bottle?

MR SHAHA says...

When you turn the water whirler upside down without spinning it, you should see that bubbles of air gurgle up through the water as it falls. The falling water blocks the hole between the two bottles, and the air in the bottom is squashed as the water takes up more and more space in the bottle. This increases the pressure in the air. Eventually, the pressure becomes great enough for some air to force its way through the water, making a bubble. The bubble releases the pressure in the bottom bottle, so the air is once again trapped until the pressure becomes high enough for more air to push its way through the water. This repeated process is what causes the water to 'glug' from the top bottle, rather than flow smoothly out.

When you spin the bottles around, the water is flung out to the sides where it continues to go around, even after you've stopped moving your hand. This is because spinning things have a tendency to keep spinning, and because there is not much friction between the water and the bottle to slow it down. As the water is also falling down the bottle at the same time as it is spinning, the water spirals down the sides of the bottle and forms a vortex. The hole in the middle of the vortex means the air from the bottom bottle can now travel up freely and the water no longer 'glugs'.

DEEP-WATER DIVER

PARTS REQUIRED

* 1 clear plastic drink bottle with lid (ideally a colourless 2-litre one, but a smaller one will work)
* 1 mug or glass
* Water
* 1 pen lid (ideally one without a hole at the top)
* Small lump of blu-tack

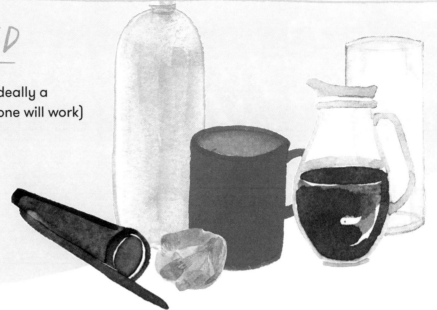

People have always wanted to explore the underwater world and have invented lots of ways to help them do it, from diving bells to scuba apparatus to submarines. The main difficulties to overcome are breathing underwater and withstanding the tremendous pressure from the weight of water above—even a few metres below the surface. Building and playing with this deep-water diver will help you to understand one of the ways submarines can move up and down in the water.

METHOD

1 If your pen lid has a hole at the top, use some blu-tack to block it up.

2 Place your pen lid in a mug or glass of water and check that it floats.

3 Take a small amount of blu-tack, roll it into a cylinder, and wrap this around the bottom end of the pen lid. The blu-tack should not cover the hole.

4 Place the pen lid back in the water, with the bottom end in first, to check whether it still floats.

5 Repeat step 3 until the pen lid floats, sticking about halfway out of the water.

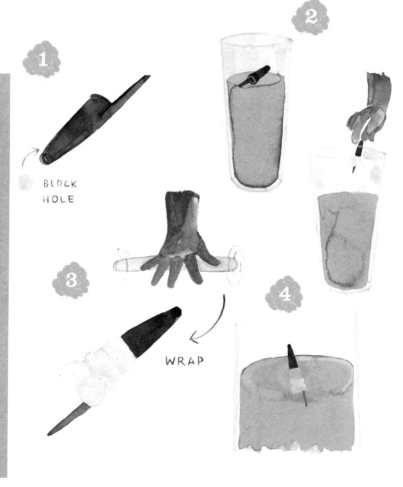

BLOCK HOLE

WRAP

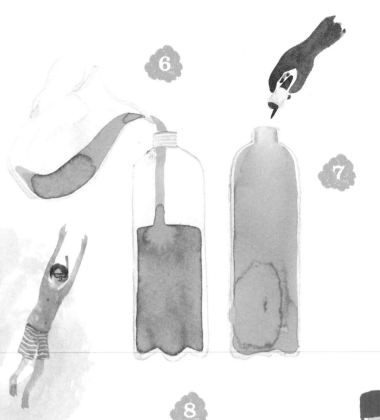

6 Completely fill your bottle with water, all the way up to the very top.

7 Carefully place the pen lid into the bottle, with the bottom end going in first. Some water will spill out. The pen lid should float but stick out a little at the top of the bottle.

8 Screw the bottle lid on tightly.

9 Using both hands, squeeze the sides of the bottle as hard as you can.

10 If your diver doesn't sink, take it out and add a bit more blu-tack to the bottom, making sure it still floats.

SQUEEZE

Can you make the diver stay **exactly in the middle** of the bottle?

Does the **size or shape** of the bottle matter?

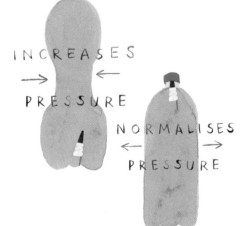

INCREASES
PRESSURE

NORMALISES
PRESSURE

Would the **temperature of the water** make a difference to how hard you have to squeeze the bottle?

To understand what's going on with the diver, we need to use the concept of 'density'. This is a way to think about how heavy something is compared to its size. Imagine two objects of the same shape and size, like a ball, but made of different materials like metal and plastic. A ball made of metal would weigh more than a ball the same size made of plastic. In other words, denser objects weigh more than less dense objects of the same shape and size.

Objects that are less dense than water will usually float, and objects that are denser than water tend to sink.

When you place your diver in the bottle, some water goes into the pen lid and traps a bubble of air inside. The diver floats because it is less dense overall than the water around it.

LESS DENSE

PLASTIC

METAL

RE DENSE

When you squeeze the bottle, you increase the pressure on the water, and this forces more of it into the pen lid. With this additional water inside, the diver becomes heavier — even though it is still the same size — so it has a bigger density. If you squeeze hard enough, enough water will go into the pen lid, and the density of the diver will become greater than the water surrounding it, so it sinks.

When you stop squeezing the bottle, the pressure goes back to normal and the extra water comes out of the pen lid. This returns the diver to its starting density, so it floats back up.

LAVA LAMP

PARTS REQUIRED

* A tall glass
* Water
* Cooking oil
* Food colouring
* One or more fizzy vitamin tablets

Not all machines have to be useful; sometimes people make things just because they are delightful. A lava lamp is one such device—it will give out some light, but its main purpose is simply to provide something mesmerising to look at. Lava lamps were invented by Edward Craven Walker after he was fascinated by an egg timer made out of two liquids that didn't mix. A real lava lamp needs electricity to work, but follow the instructions below and you can make a lava lamp that will keep you transfixed for ages.

METHOD

1 Fill your glass about a fifth of the way up with water.

2 Carefully pour the cooking oil into the glass so that you have roughly three times as much oil as water (the glass will be about four-fifths full).

3 If the oil and water have become mixed up, wait until they separate.

4 Slowly add a few drops of food colouring and wait for the water to become evenly coloured. Give the mixture a stir if the colour doesn't spread quickly enough for you.

! BE SAFE

Do not eat the fizzy vitamin tablets. Do not drink the contents of the lava lamp.

What would happen if you broke the tablet up into **smaller pieces** before dropping them into the glass?

5 Break the tablet in half and drop it into the oil.

6 Add more pieces of tablet if you want more bubbles.

7 Once you're finished playing with the lava lamp, leave it to settle overnight and then carefully pour the oil into a separate container so that you can use it for cooking.

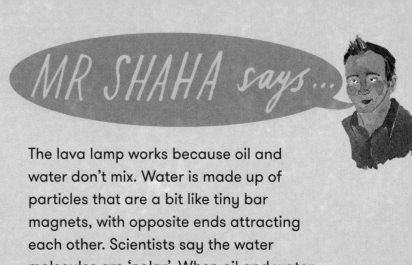

MR SHAHA says...

The lava lamp works because oil and water don't mix. Water is made up of particles that are a bit like tiny bar magnets, with opposite ends attracting each other. Scientists say the water molecules are 'polar'. When oil and water are mixed, they eventually separate because the water particles are more strongly attracted to each other than they are to the oil particles, which are not polar.

WE ARE POLAR!

OPPOSITES ATTRACT!

WATER MOLECULES H_2O

The oil ends up floating on the water, even if you put it in the container first. This is because oil is less dense than water, which means that if you have the same amount of oil and water, the oil will weigh less.

When you drop a piece of tablet into the lava lamp, it does not react with the oil but instead falls straight down into the water. When it hits the water, it starts to dissolve and releases chemicals that react to produce carbon-dioxide gas. This makes bubbles in the water. The bubbles are less dense than both water and oil, so they float upwards, taking some of the coloured water with them. Once they reach the top of the container, the bubbles burst, and the coloured water falls back down.

BEWILDERING BEAN

PARTS REQUIRED

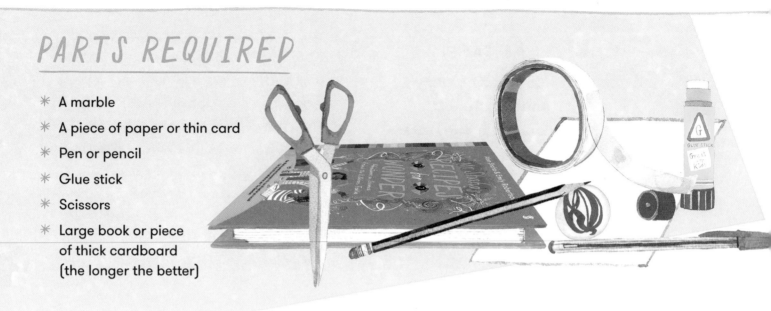

* A marble
* A piece of paper or thin card
* Pen or pencil
* Glue stick
* Scissors
* Large book or piece of thick cardboard (the longer the better)

I'd heard of Mexican jumping beans when I was a child, but had never actually seen one until many years later when I looked them up on YouTube. These 'beans' are still sold as toys in some parts of the world, and as you would expect from their name, they move around on their own—sometimes even jumping up into the air. The secret to their mysterious movement is that they're not actually beans, but seed pods with a tiny caterpillar inside. The bean you'll make for this activity is not alive, but you'll still be able to baffle some people with the way it moves.

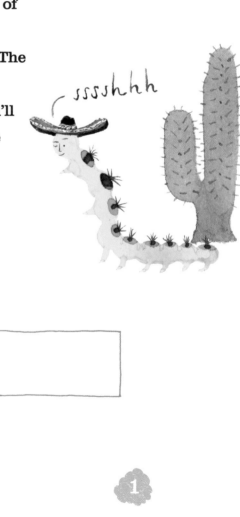

sssshhh

TRACE ME

1

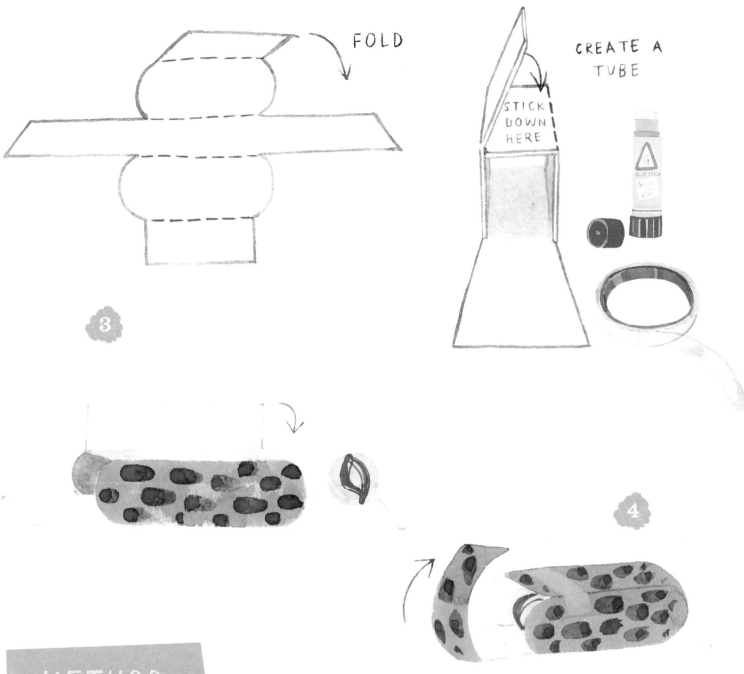

FOLD

CREATE A
TUBE

STICK
DOWN
HERE

③

④

METHOD

1 Copy or trace the bean template onto your piece of paper and cut out the shape. If your paper doesn't let you see through it to trace the bean template, try copying or print it out from **alomshaha.com/machines**. This template will work for a standard marble, but if your marble is bigger or smaller, just copy the template and change its size so that the width of each section of the template is slightly (about 1 mm) bigger than your marble.

2 If you want to, you can decorate your bean at this stage.

3 Fold along the dotted lines and glue the two short tabs together to form a rectangular tube. Check that your marble fits inside this tube and can move about freely.

4 Keeping your marble in the tube, wrap the long tab of paper round and stick it so that the marble is completely enclosed in the bean.

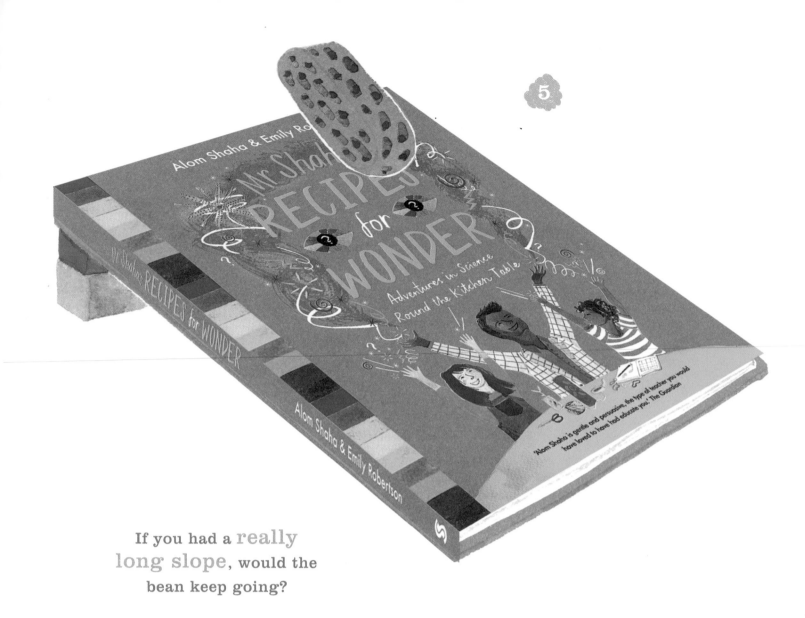

5

If you had a **really long slope**, would the bean keep going?

Does the bean work on **different** surfaces?

6

5 Place your bean on a book or piece of cardboard and gently tilt it until the bean starts moving. With a bit of practice, you should be able to get the bean to repeatedly flip over all the way down the slope.

6 Try playing with the bean in the palm of your hand and see if you can get it to look 'alive'.

What happens if you **change the angle** of your slope?

What would happen if you made your bean **longer** or **shorter?**

TA-DAA

WOW

AMAZING BEAN SHOW

MR SHAHA says...

For anyone who doesn't know there's a marble inside, the bewildering bean may seem to have a life of its own. The bean flip-flops its way down a slope because of the way the marble inside it rolls downwards and then hits the closed end of the bean. At this point, the marble is slowed down, but the curved shape of the bean means it doesn't completely come to a stop. Instead, the friction between the marble and the paper allows the rolling marble to grip the paper in front of it and pull it downwards, causing the bean to flip over. Once the bean is flipped, the marble can roll freely again. This process repeats itself, making the bean flip over and over for as long as it stays on a slope.

EASY ELECTROMAGNET

PARTS REQUIRED

* About a metre of insulated wire (you can get this from an unused power cable or phone charger).
* A stainless-steel dessert spoon or fork
* 1 AA battery (Caution: DO NOT use a rechargeable battery!)
* Sticky tape
* Metal paperclips
* Scissors or wire stripper

Magnets seem magical—they will attract or repel each other and are delightful to play with. Magnets are also really useful, not just for sticking stuff to the fridge, but for lots of technology like loudspeakers, hairdryers, and doorbells. In this activity, you'll learn how to turn an ordinary piece of cutlery into a magnet that you can turn on and off. After making your own electromagnet, you should be able to see how engineers can make magnets that are strong enough to lift cars and trucks in a scrapyard.

The wire in this activity can get hot if you connect it to the battery for too long, so disconnect the wire immediately if this happens. Fine wires can prick your fingers and can also become very hot very quickly, so follow the instructions carefully to avoid this happening.

BE SAFE

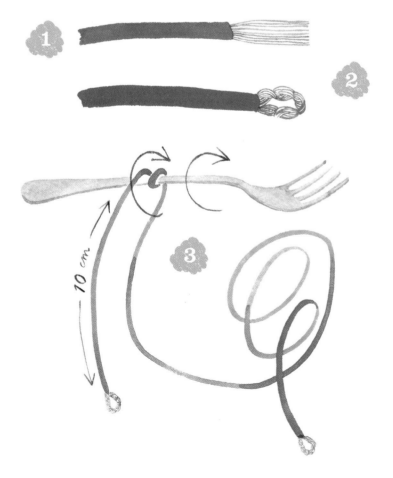

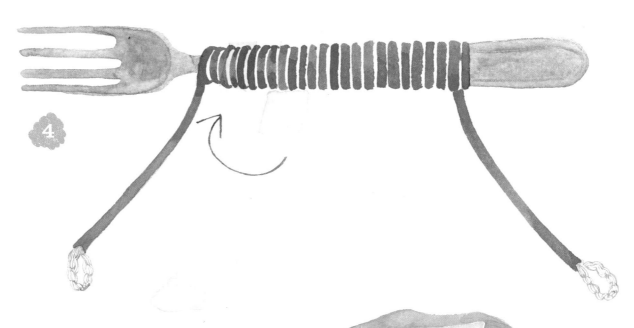

4

Can you devise an experiment to test how the number of times you wrap the wire around the fork or spoon handle **affects the strength** of the electromagnet?

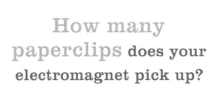

5

6

How many **paperclips** does your electromagnet pick up?

METHOD

1 Strip about 2 cm of the insulation off the ends of your wire using a wire stripper, or by gently cutting round the plastic with scissors.

2 If the uninsulated wire is made up of lots of fine wires, twist these firmly together to make one thick braid of wire. Twist this into a flat loop.

3 Starting about 10 cm from one end of the wire, coil the wire tightly around the handle of your spoon or fork. Do not overlap the coils, and leave about 10 cm of uncoiled wire at the end.

4 Wrap some sticky tape around the coils of wire so that they stay in place.

5 Use your thumb and pointer finger to press each end of the wire against opposite ends of the battery.

6 With your other hand, pick up the head of your spoon or fork and use the bottom end of the handle to magnetically pick up the paperclips.

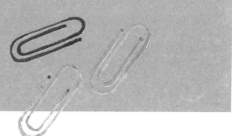

How could you investigate whether changing the thickness of your electromagnet's core affects its strength?

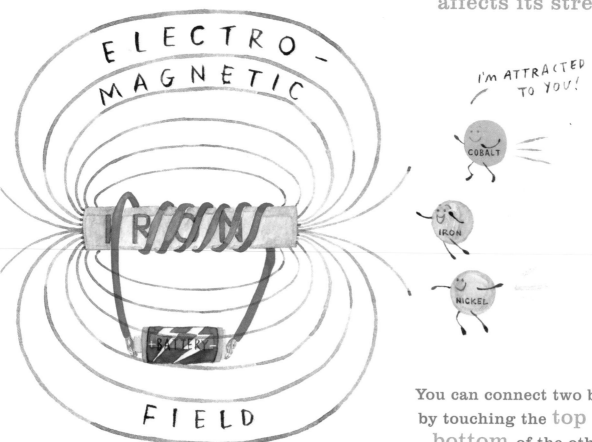

ELECTRO-MAGNETIC

I'M ATTRACTED TO YOU!

COBALT

IRON

NICKEL

FIELD

BATTERY

You can connect two batteries together by touching the top of one to the bottom of the other. How do you think using two or more batteries connected like this would affect the strength of the electromagnet?

MR SHAHA says...

The space around a magnet, in which another magnet is pushed or pulled, is called a magnetic field. Some metals like iron, nickel, and cobalt will also be pulled towards a magnet if they are in its magnetic field. A permanent magnet, like a fridge magnet, has a magnetic field that is always there around the magnet.

When an electrical current flows through a wire, it produces a magnetic field around the wire. Stopping the current makes the magnetic field disappear. This shows that electricity and magnetism are two aspects of the same thing, which scientists call electromagnetism.

Wrapping the wire into a coil around an iron core increases the strength of the magnetic field produced by the current in the wire. An electromagnet can be more useful than a permanent magnet because it can be switched on and off, and its strength can be increased or decreased by changing the current in the wire or the number of turns when it is coiled.

BALANCING BIRD

PARTS REQUIRED

* 1 piece of scrap card from a cereal box or similar
* 1 piece of tracing paper or thin sheet of plain paper
* Pen or pencil
* 2 small coins of the same type
* Scissors
* A roll of sticky tape or masking tape
* Glue stick

As a science teacher, I often use toys in my lessons to demonstrate scientific principles in action. One of my favourites is the 'balancing bird', which seems to defy gravity and go against all our intuition about how things should balance. I hope you'll find this toy as delightful as my students do, and that making your own helps you to learn about how it works so you can go on to design and make other balancing toys.

METHOD

1 Trace the bird outline on the next page of this book onto your piece of paper. If your paper doesn't let you see through it to trace the bird, try copying or print it out from **alomshaha.com/machines**.

2 Using the glue stick, stick the paper onto your piece of cardboard.

3 Cut the bird out of the cardboard and decorate it however you want.

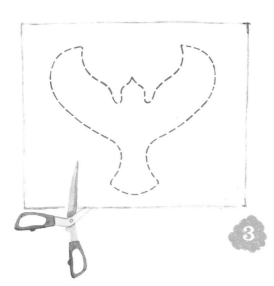

Can you make your own **balancing butterfly** or other shape?

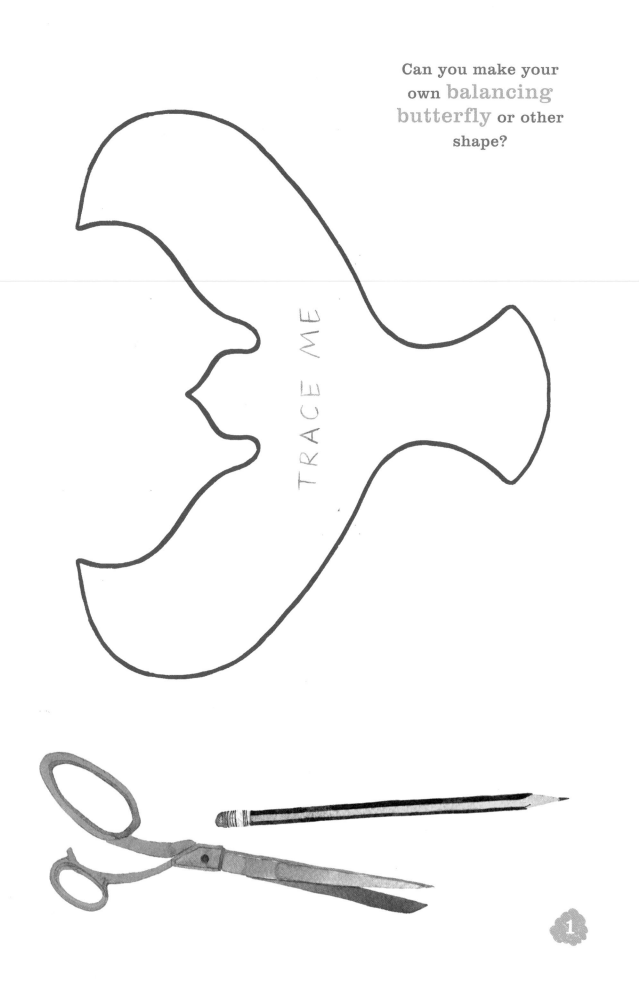

TRACE ME

58

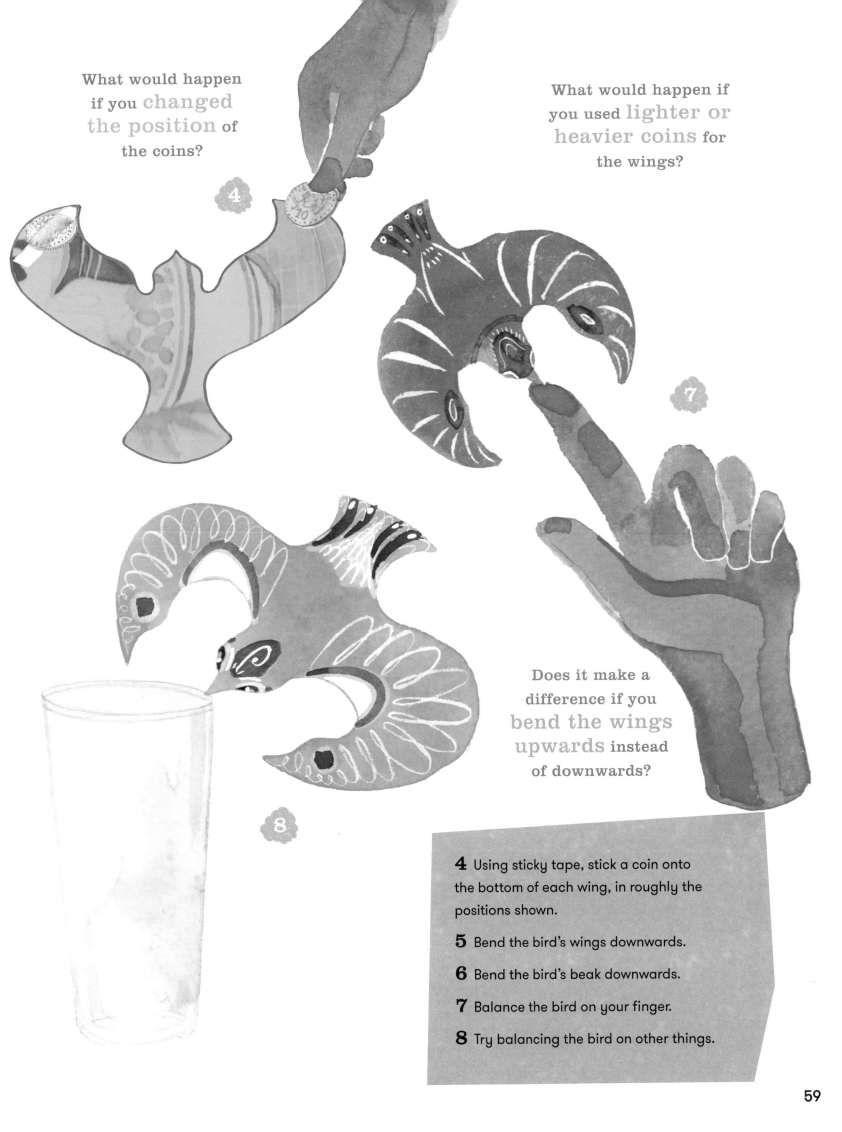

What would happen if you **changed the position** of the coins?

What would happen if you used **lighter or heavier coins** for the wings?

Does it make a difference if you **bend the wings upwards** instead of downwards?

4 Using sticky tape, stick a coin onto the bottom of each wing, in roughly the positions shown.

5 Bend the bird's wings downwards.

6 Bend the bird's beak downwards.

7 Balance the bird on your finger.

8 Try balancing the bird on other things.

MR SHAHA says...

If you try to balance an object like a plate or a pencil, you'll find that there's only one point on the object below which you can put your finger to keep it stable. Scientists call this point the 'centre of mass' or 'centre of gravity' of the object. You can think of it as the point around which the

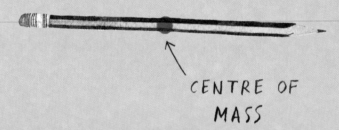

CENTRE OF
MASS

mass or weight of an object is evenly distributed. With something like a plate or pencil, the centre of mass is roughly in the middle of the object. For something that is heavier on one side, like a hammer, the centre of mass will be closer to the heavier end. The centre of mass doesn't have to be part of the object itself — for example, the centre of mass of a roll of sticky tape or a coat hanger is in the middle of the hole.

An object can only be balanced if its centre of mass stays in the same vertical line as the point at which it is pivoted, otherwise it will start to turn. If the centre of mass is above the pivot, this turning will make the object fall over. You can see this for yourself by trying to balance a roll of sticky tape on top of your finger — it's

CENTRE OF
MASS

hard to do because the centre of mass doesn't stay above the pivot.

If the centre of mass of an object is below the pivot point, and it is moved, it will always turn in a way that brings the centre of mass back below the pivot. Again, you can see this for yourself by balancing a coat hanger on your finger by the tip of its hook — if you move the hanger to one side, it will swing back to its stable position. This is the secret to the stability of the balancing bird — it is made so that its centre of mass is below the point at which it is supported (its beak), and the centre of mass always falls back to a position directly below the pivot if it is moved.

You can change the centre of mass of the bird by changing the position of the coins or by adjusting the angle at which you bend the wings. If you want the bird to balance, most of its weight needs to be below the pivot point.

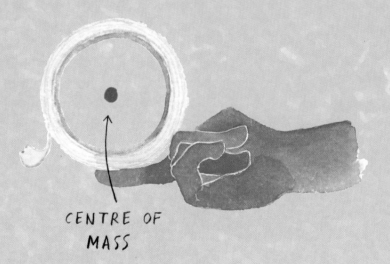

CENTRE OF
MASS

HANDY HARMONICA

PARTS REQUIRED

* 2 wooden ice-lolly sticks (clean and dry)
* 1 wide rubber band
* 4 small rubber bands
* 1 piece of scrap paper
* Scissors

According to NASA, the first musical instruments ever taken into space were a harmonica and some jingle bells. Astronauts Walter Schirra and Tom Stafford smuggled the instruments on board the Gemini VI spacecraft in December 1965 and used them to play a surprise rendition of the Christmas song 'Jingle Bells' for a radio transmission back to earth. You might not get the chance to take this home-made harmonica into space, but with a bit of practice, you might be able to play a song or two to surprise your friends and family.

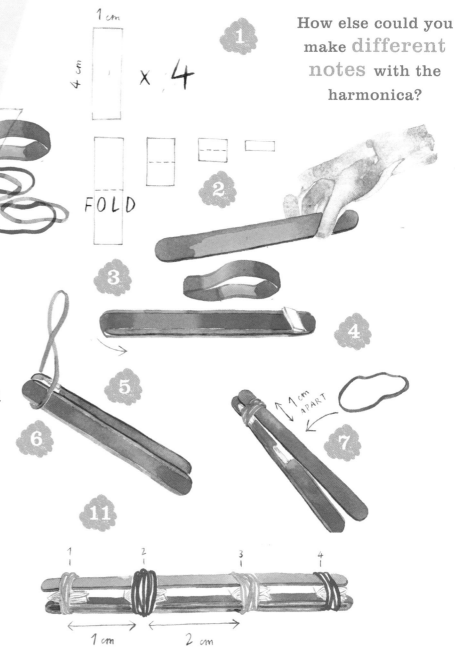

How else could you make **different notes** with the harmonica?

METHOD

1 Cut your scrap paper into four pieces that are roughly 4 cm by 1 cm big.

2 Fold each piece of paper in half along its length three times so you are left with a folded piece of paper roughly 1 cm by ½ cm. Keep these to one side.

3 Stretch the wide rubber band lengthwise over one of the ice-lolly sticks.

4 Place one of your folded bits of paper on top of the rubber band at one end of the ice-lolly stick.

5 Put the other stick on top so that the piece of paper is sandwiched between the sticks.

6 Wrap a small rubber band around the paper and ice-lolly sticks so that the piece of paper is held firmly in place.

Does blowing **soft or hard** change the sound?

When you blow into the harmonica, you make the rubber band vibrate. The vibrations of the rubber band are passed on to the air around, making sound waves that travel outwards and eventually into your ears. You can feel these vibrations with your fingertips where you hold the harmonica, and you can see the rubber band vibrating if you look in a mirror while blowing.

You get a different pitch of sound depending on which hole you blow into because the different lengths of rubber sandwiched between the paper dividers vibrate differently. Shorter bits of rubber vibrate more quickly (with a higher frequency) and produce a higher note. Stretching the rubber band more tightly will also change the way it vibrates — a more tightly stretched rubber band will produce a higher note. Can you design and make a harmonica that only has one hole between two dividers, but allows you to make different notes?

7 Place a second bit of folded paper in between the ice-lolly sticks so that there is a gap of about 1 cm between it and the first piece of paper. Again, cut off any paper sticking out from between the sticks.

8 Use another small elastic band to hold that piece of paper in place.

9 Repeat with another piece of paper placed about 2 cm along, and then with the final piece of paper placed right at the other end of the ice-lolly sticks.

10 With the rubber band side of your harmonica facing downwards, blow through the gaps between the paper dividers.

11 If the harmonica doesn't sound quite right, try moving the positions of the spacers.

Does the harmonica **feel different** in your fingers when you blow through the different notes?

ACKNOWLEDGEMENTS

This was such a fun book to write! Thank you to Emily for capturing the joy of making these machines in her beautiful illustrations.

A massive thank you to my agent Catherine Clarke and the team at Scribble—Philip Gwyn Jones, Miriam Rosenbloom, Sarah Braybrooke, Kate O'Donnell, Molly Slight, and Tess Cullity—for doing all the wonderful things they do to make an idea into a book.

I spent a summer making and trying out all the machines, and there are a whole bunch of people who helped me get them right and think about how they worked—thank you Helen Czerski, Dean Burnett, Michael de Podesta, Paul McCrory, Alby Reid, David Sang, Andrea Sella, Alex Weatherall, and Joe Wright.

Special thanks to Jonathan Sanderson and Carol Davenport of NUSTEM for allowing me to use their mini mangonel design.

Gill Fletcher looked after Renu and Mina, her grandchildren, for long periods of time when I was writing the book, and I couldn't have managed without her help. Thank you, Gill.

Finally, thank you to Kate Fletcher, who helps make my life marvellous in countless ways.

—Alom Shaha

To download activity sheets,
watch instructional videos,
and join the community
of wondermiths, visit:
www.alomshaha.com/machines

ALSO AVAILABLE

Learn about sound by making wine glasses sing,
investigate chemical reactions with vitamin-powered
rockets, and explore Newton's Third Law by making
balloon-driven cars. All you need are a few simple
items from your kitchen cupboards — and the power
of curiosity! Every child can be a scientist with the
help of Mr Shaha and his recipes for wonder!